21-Day Devotional:

Finding Peace During the Healing Process

21-Day Devotional:

Finding Peace During the Healing Process

Scripture quotations are taken from the Holy Bible, New International Version, NIV Copyright 1973, 1978, 1984, 2011 by Biblica, Inc. Used by permission. All rights reserved worldwide.

Scripture quotations are taken from the Holy Bible, New Living Translation, copyright 1996, 2004, 2015 by Tyndale House Foundation. Used by permission of Tyndale House Publishers, a Division of Tyndale House Ministries, Carol Stream, Illinois 60188. All rights reserved.

Scripture quotations marked MSG are taken from THE MESSAGE, copyright 1993, 2002, 2018 by Eugene H. Peterson. Used by permission of NavPress. All rights reserved. Represented by Tyndale House Publishers, a Division of Tyndale House Ministries.

Scripture quotations marked (TLB) are taken from The Living Bible copyright 1971. Used by permission of Tyndale House Publishers, a Division of Tyndale House Ministries, Carol Stream, Illinois 60188. All rights reserved.

Scripture quotations are taken from the ESV Bible (The Holy Bible, English Standard Version), copyright 2001 by Crossway Bibles, a publishing ministry of Good News Publishers. Used by permission. All rights reserved.

Two definition quotations are taken from Merriam-Websters Dictionary Online Copyright 2019. Used by permission. All rights reserved.

No part of this publication may be reproduced, stored in a retrieval system, or transmitted in any form or by any means, electronic, mechanical, photocopying, recording, scanning, or otherwise without the prior written permission of the Author. Requests to the Author for permissions should be submitted to Cassidy Lee at the following email address: ConsultantCassidy@gmail.com.

Copyright 2020

Cassidy Lee

All rights reserved.

ISBN: 978-0-578-76745-1

Foreword
by Lorena Crook

It was a great honor for me to be asked by Cassidy to write a foreword for her book of devotional and inspirational readings. I've watched her over the years, fine-tuning what she loved to do. She was diligent in developing her skills to share her thoughts and perspectives about life with others.

Reading has been her great love from the time she could form and speak her first words. She became a passionate reader, knowing early on, she was going to allow that passion to take her to many places. She let it open avenues to meet people from varied backgrounds and ways of living.

I am so proud of you, Cassidy. It has been my great joy as your grandmother to see how your love for reading has been beneficial to thousands of your students and has spilled over into your spiritual life.

I pray for continued success with your special gift. Remember, the Gifter sees your gift; He, too, approves of what you are doing with it.

How to Use this Devotional:

As with all things, the proper approach will reap the desired results. Throughout this devotional, you may see order and focus mentioned quite often. It is because these two factors create the conditions for the guidance in this devotional to take root and bear fruit.

I.) Create a reading schedule and get organized/declutter.
Schedule a daily time for reading the devotional after reading your Bible. This devotional is in no way meant as a substitute for the Word of God. It is a supplement.

II.) Pay attention to your diet and exercise.
Pay closer attention to your diet and exercise habits. Adapt them based on your health needs for a reset. Our bodies can only perform at the optimal output when we concern ourselves with the quality of input. In short, when we feel good, we get good results.

IIIII.) Journal your thoughts.
Feel free to jot down notes, insights, or thoughts as you read. Journaling will act as a way for you to reflect on your revelations. It is a record of your revelations when you need to remind yourself of your progress.

IVIV.) Be consistent.
Whether it is with the devotional or anything in life, consistency is vital. We cannot expect changes in ourselves if the work put in is unstable and lukewarm at best. Remember, it takes 21 days to form a new pattern.

Day One

Hurt and Betrayal

Scriptures: John 13:30, 2 Samuel 3:27, Proverbs 4:15-17, Proverbs 4:25-27

"Fools make fun of guilt, but the godly acknowledge it and seek reconciliation" (Proverbs 14:9, NLT).

Observation: Betrayal leaves a deep wound. It is caused when our trust is violated. We feel compromised. We are no longer safe. Sometimes we retreat into ourselves, trying to find safety in blocking it all out. Betrayal creates an ache inside our hearts that is slow to heal.

Only God's grace can eliminate the trauma of our negative experiences. Instead of trying to mask our hurt, we should be utterly transparent with Him, so He can fully heal and deliver us from the pain caused by our afflictions.

A constant state of confession to God can allow us a deep cleansing of our hearts.

Application: Consider releasing the people or circumstances that have caused you pain. Write it out and throw it away if you're not able to speak with the people who've directly caused you harm. Sometimes you just have to move forward, with or without an apology.

Prayer: Father, help me to be transparent about my feelings of hurt and betrayal. Give me the strength and the wisdom to release my pain. Only You can help me to operate in love and forgiveness. I want to be free and whole again. In Jesus' name, amen.

Day Two

Supplanting Anger

Scriptures: "May the Lord judge between us. Perhaps the Lord will punish you for what you are trying to do to me, but I will never harm you" (1 Samuel 24:12, NLT.

"The Lord himself will fight for you. Just stay calm" (Exodus 14:14, NLT).

"Hatred stirs up quarrels, but love makes up for all offenses" (Proverbs 10:12, NLT).

Observation: Due to its ability to catalyze a plethora of emotions, betrayal can send us into a downward spiral. A betrayal leads to hurt. Our hurt turns into a deep depression. Then almost overnight, our depression blossoms into anger. Anger creates a sensitive yet volatile place in our hearts. Its roots are deep and spread to areas we never thought would be adversely affected. Never underestimate how these emotions can feed off each other and cause an endless cycle. The cycle of emotions must be broken by supplanting the anger that initially sprung up from betrayal.

Walking in a constant state of deliverance is a process. We must rely on the power of God to purify us because we are fighting otherworldly opposition.

Application: Consider examining your perspective on the matter that angers you. Then, flip the script on it. Find the positive and use it to maintain a sense of peace within yourself. You cannot change how certain events play out, but you can change how you react to them. Build emotional control.

Prayer: Father, I know anger is not of You. Please take my anger and replace it with peace. I ask You to bring insight and understanding into the situation. Transform my perspective. Make it an opportunity for growth and not regression. In Jesus' name, amen.

Day Three

Overcoming Offense

Scriptures: Ephesians 4:31-32

"Don't be misled you cannot mock the justice of God. You will always harvest what you plant. Those who live only to satisfy their sinful nature will harvest decay and death from that sinful nature. But those who live to please the Spirit will harvest everlasting life from the Spirit" (Galatians 6:7-8, NLT).

"Hiding hatred makes you a liar; slandering others makes you a fool" (Proverbs 10:18, NLT).

"An offended friend is harder to win back than a fortified city. Arguments separate friends like a gate locked with bars" (Proverbs 18:19, NLT).

Observation: The feeling of helplessness often follows when we endure an offense. At other times, the thoughts of wanting to respond negatively to the offense are at the forefront of our minds. Yet there is one thing we must always remember: God will hold people accountable for the offense and deceit they commit. It's one of the many sureties in life. I've learned to rest in that truth. "Beloved, never avenge yourselves, but leave it to the wrath of God, for it is written, 'Vengeance is mine, I will repay, says the Lord'" (Romans 12:19). He will repay. He does so in such a seamless way; it supersedes any conceivable reprimand or punishment a person could concoct. He intimately knows the oppressor just as he knows the person who is oppressed.

Find peace in His boundless wisdom. Find rest in His plans.

Application: Reflect on what offended you. Ask yourself if you are offended because of where the offense comes from or because it is an insecurity of yours that was targeted. If it is an insecurity, speak positive affirmations over yourself. Your goal should be to conquer the vulnerability, so it is no longer a target area. If you are offended by the source, consider speaking frankly with the person and inform him or her of how the offense affected you.

Prayer: Father, blot out the offenses I've endured. Erase them from my heart and mind. Show me how to overcome these offenses before they cause me to stumble. Forgive me for any offense(s) I may have caused those around me. In Jesus' name, amen.

Day Four

Investing in Relationships

Scriptures: "Love prospers when a fault is forgiven but dwelling on it separates close friends" (Proverbs 17:9, NLT).

"A friend is always loyal, and a brother is born to help in time of need" (Proverbs 17:17, NLT).

"There are 'friends' who destroy each other, but a real friend sticks closer than a brother" (Proverbs 18:24, NLT).

"Dear friends, let us continue to love one another, for love comes from God. Anyone who loves is a child of God and knows God" (1 John 4:7, NLT).

Observation: How many times have you found yourself wondering if someone is genuinely concerned about your best interests? Now, how many times have you asked yourself if you're worried about someone else's best interests? Relationships are organic. If you do not feed them, they will wither and die.

Most people value loyalty, dependability, and stability in their relationships. No one wants to be around a person incapable of keeping commitments, no matter what those commitments may be. Ask yourself if you are living up to these qualities in your relationships with other people as well.

Much reflection is needed to evaluate if relationships are healthy and meeting their full potential. Time should be spent deciding how to enact a plan to appropriately respond to the outcome of your reflection.

Remember, if love is conditional or finite, it is not truly love. Learn the difference and accept the reality.

Application: Make a list. Write down the pros and cons of the relationships you find yourself questioning. Also, write down the bonds that cause you the most heartache. Once you establish the pros and cons, determine if the cons are due to misunderstandings and if the pros are due to you overlooking things about the relationship which make you uncomfortable. Pray about how to confront the other person in each of these relationships. Do not maintain a relationship with someone that is unhealthy, but don't throw away relationships simply because they are not easily navigated. As stated earlier, sometimes friction means it is time for you to grow.

Prayer: Father, bring to light the relationships that are of Your will. If they are toxic and delay my maturity into the person You have called me to be, please break their hold on my life. Give me discernment for the relationships that will inevitably bring You the most glory. In Jesus' name, amen.

Day Five

Rallied by Purpose

Scriptures: "For we are God's masterpiece. He has created us anew in Christ Jesus, so we can do the good things He planned for us long ago" (Ephesians 2:10, NLT).

"The generous will prosper; those who refresh others will themselves be refreshed" (Proverbs 11:25, NLT).

"The seeds of good deeds become a tree of life; a wise person wins friends" (Proverbs 11:30, NLT).

"Giving a gift can open doors; it gives access to important people!" (Proverbs 18:16, NLT)

Observation: Work done for the Kingdom of God is imperishable. Each person has a God-given mission only he or she can fulfill. Therefore, the pursuit of purpose brings fulfillment.

The necessity of our purpose far outweighs the hardships we endure to fulfill said purpose. Besides, the blessing of our mission affects others and is the bigger picture. Our focus must remain higher than our current circumstances.

When the grand picture is in perspective, insight begins to overshadow the discouragement that often accompanies the obstacles we face. So, allow the insight you gain to rejuvenate you and rally your sense of purpose.

Application: Consider your natural talents and interests. Typically, we are drawn to the things we are purposed to do, and we have a natural affinity for them. Ask yourself if what you are doing aligns with the Word of God. If it does, pursue it with gusto.

Prayer: Father, You have fully equipped me for my purpose. I will instinctively know what to do when the time is right. I declare and decree I am a masterpiece (Ephesians 2:10, NLT), fit to do a good work for the Lord. In Jesus' name, amen.

Day Six

Fighting to the End

Scripture: "So I run straight to the goal with purpose in every step. I fight to win. I'm not just shadowboxing or playing around. Like an athlete I punish my body, mistreating it, training it to do what it should, not what it wants to. Otherwise I fear that after enlisting others for the race, I might be declared unfit and ordered to stand aside" (Corinthians 9:26-27, TLB).

Observation: ".... I fight to win" (Corinthians 9:26, TLB). I have never heard of a person going into a fight with the absolute desire to lose. Deep down, we all hold out hope we will face a challenge and come out of it victorious. The best practice for arising as the victor is to train, to stay ready. Dedicated athletes do not spend their downtime between events lounging around and neglecting their training. They train for their next opponent. They prepare for what is to come. So, let us be like athletes. Let us discipline ourselves.

We admire athletes for their achievements, yet we fail to realize the amount of work that goes into those achievements. If they do not keep up the necessary preparations or choose to use shortcuts, they will be disqualified. May we keep in mind how others are watching and admiring our life's work. Let us not disqualify ourselves by seeking shortcuts or by neglecting our training.

There is one sure thing: we control our actions. While we may not fully anticipate or control the future, we can control whether we are prepared for it.

Application: Become more organized. Sometimes the feeling of being overwhelmed causes us to fall behind in our regular regimen. Also, consider asking others for help. We are encouraged by others, and the synergy it creates can rejuvenate us when we are feeling depleted from the drain of everyday work.

Prayer: Father, strengthen the warrior spirit within me. You have not given me a spirit of fear but of power, love, and a sound mind (II Timothy 1-17). Your Son made the ultimate sacrifice so that I could receive this life in abundance (John 10:10). I make a declaration starting today; I will fight without ceasing to experience the fullness of the life You've given me. In Jesus' name, amen.

Day Seven

Freedom in Contentment

Scriptures: "I am not saying this because I am in need, for I have learned to be content whatever the circumstances. I know what it is to be in need, and I know what it is to have plenty. I have learned the secret of being content in any and every situation, whether well fed or hungry, whether living in plenty or in want. I can do all this through Him who gives me strength" (Philippians 4:11-13, NIV).

"Better to be patient than powerful; better to have self-control than to conquer a city. We may throw the dice, but the Lord determines how they fall" (Proverbs 16:32-33, NLT).

"Be thankful in all circumstances, for this is God's will for you who belong to Christ Jesus" (1 Thessalonians 5:18, NLT).

Observation: Life has enough difficulties without us being obsessed with future events. We forge on through each day, hoping the next will be better. Yet we miss the freeing feeling of being content with our current circumstances. It does not mean we do not want better things if we are striving for needed improvements; however, it does mean we should not hold ourselves to unrealistic standards. Imperfections are normal and found in all of us. When we accept them and move forward, we free ourselves of the burden of perfection.

Contentment is not the same as complacency. Complacency causes us not to expect the best effort from ourselves. Contentment causes us to rest easy even when things are in transition or unforeseeable. Contentment saves us from rushing ahead and causing disaster when simply being patient can yield the best results. Learn to see the upside to contentment and re-frame it.

Application: Ponder how you may have created issues where there were no issues. Meditate on the things you do have instead of the things you do not have. You will experience peace of mind when you concentrate on the here and now, instead of launching yourself into the future.

Prayer: Father, please show me how to be content with what I have and not worry over what is to come. Help me to stay in the moment and refuse to let the cares of the world weigh me down. There is freedom in contentment. I ask you to guide me and show me how to discover freedom every day. In Jesus' name, amen.

Day Eight

Being Thankful for the Bad Times

Scriptures: 1 Corinthians 12:9, Romans 8:35-39, Romans 15:4

"We are pressed on every side by troubles, but we are not crushed. We are perplexed but not driven to despair. We are hunted down but never abandoned by God. We get knocked down, but we are not destroyed"

(2 Corinthians 4:8-9, NLT).

Observation: I'll be the first to admit I'm not always grateful. The storms of life can sometimes hinder my ability to operate in a spirit of thankfulness. Yet I realize how bad things could be. There are levels of despair. I know quite well how traumatic events can stack up against each other. I've compared them to each other and thought, "At least it's not as bad as two years ago."

Perspective is key. I focus my vision through a different lens. It will not happen overnight. It must become a habit. Once it's a habit, you can combat the negativity that usually follows not operating in thankfulness.

Application: Make a list of things you are thankful for. Keep it handy, and use it to remind yourself when you're having trouble recalling anything. Go a step further and compose a list of things consisting of your 'highlight reel.' Your highlight reel is a list of obstacles you've overcome in the past. Use it as a reminder of your strength to endure. If you survived those other circumstances, you can survive your current ordeal.

Prayer: Father, help me to recall the good times, so they outweigh the bad. Help me to have a cheerful, grateful heart during adversity. I have weathered other storms, and I trust You to help me weather this one. In Jesus' name, amen.

Day Nine

Being Thankful for the Good Times

Scriptures: "This is the day the Lord has made. We will rejoice and be glad in it" (Psalms 118:24, NLT).

"The Lord is my rock, my fortress, and my savior; my God is my rock, in whom I find protection. He is my shield, the power that saves me, and my place of safety" (Psalms 18:2, NLT).

"The Lord is my strength and my shield; my heart trusts in Him, and He helps me. My heart leaps for joy, and with my song I praise Him" (Psalms 28:7, NIV).

Observation: Out of sight, out of mind. Occasionally, that is our attitude towards God during good times. The level of gratitude changes. At times we feel entitled to our good times, our times of prosperity. Instead, we should realize how blessed we are and the magnitude of experiencing a season of peace. Not all times will be peaceful and prosperous. Therefore, the good times should be cherished, and genuine expressions of thankfulness should be issued forth to God.

Application: Spend at least five minutes in daily prayer, focusing on gratefulness. Even the things often viewed as inconsequential should be received with thankfulness.

Prayer: Father, You are great in all Your mercy, even in the little things. Please help me to be mindful and recall Your loving kindness during times of peace. Help me to maintain a spirit of gratefulness knowing such peace should not be taken for granted. In Jesus' name, amen.

Day Ten

Seeking Validation from Others

Scriptures: "A peaceful heart leads to a healthy body; jealousy is like cancer in the bones" (Proverbs 14:30, NLT).

Observation: Your contributions to the world are unique. If you did not exist, neither would your contributions. The world is made richer because of your existence. Therefore, it is illogical to seek to please others. Their stamp of approval will not make or break your purpose. While affirmation strengthens, empowers, and pushes us to move forward, it should not be the foundation on which our identity is built.

Application: When you encounter the need to seek approval from others or measure your worth against the people around you, remind yourself how there is only one of *you*. Only *you* were born with your gifts and purposes.

Prayer: Father, help me find joy in who I am. Help me to run my race and keep my focus from drifting to how others are running their races. In Jesus' name, amen.

Day Eleven

The Importance of Self-Care

Scriptures: "Before daybreak the next morning, Jesus got up and went out to an isolated place to pray" (Mark 1:35, NLT).

"Then Jesus said, 'Let's go off by ourselves to a quiet place and rest awhile.' He said this because there were so many people coming and going that Jesus and His apostles didn't even have time to eat. So, they left by boat for a quiet place, where they could be alone" (Mark 6:31-32, NLT).

"Don't you realize that your body is the temple of the Holy Spirit, who lives in you and was given to you by God? You do not belong to yourself, for God bought you with a high price. So, you must honor God with your body" (1 Corinthians 6:19-20, NLT).

Observation: Knowing when and how to bow out of a situation gracefully is an art form. It requires wisdom and experience. Bowing out of things should not make you feel guilty or inadequate. Learn to know the difference between being lazy and self-preservation. Oftentimes people who possess giving hearts are overextended by the people around them. Whether those people are aware of their actions or not, it is up to the giver to learn the empowerment that comes from using the word, "no." Your "no" should bring finality to any coercion from individuals seeking to drain you of energy reserved for God, yourself, and your loved ones.

If you're still unconvinced, take into account the validity of the statement, "You cannot pour from an empty vessel." Your wellbeing should be important to the people around you, the same way their wellbeing is important to you. If they do not share your feelings, it's time to reevaluate the relationship.

(See "Day 4: Investing in Relationships" for a recap).

Application: Be more mindful of your spiritual, emotional, mental, and physical health. Daily prayer and reflection are vital. Pay closer attention to your health as well. Positively altering your sleeping and eating habits will reap immediate results. The world has created numerous ways to invade our private lives. Make it a priority to enforce firm boundaries and apply the basic tenets of self-care.

Prayer: Father, please give me the strength and confidence to stand my ground and reclaim my time. By your Holy Spirit, please lift my spirit when I am feeling low. Help me to acknowledge that pouring from an empty cup only leads to further setbacks. I praise You for giving me everything I need and more. In Jesus' name, amen.

Day Twelve

Valuing Wisdom

Scriptures: "Doing wrong is fun for a fool but living wisely brings pleasure to the sensible" (Proverbs 10:23, NLT).

"Gray hair is a crown of glory; it is gained by living a godly life" (Proverbs 16:31, NLT).

Observation: There are some people we meet in life who never need to 'learn their lessons the hard way.' They have an innate ability to make sensible decisions, even in the tensest situations. Frequently, it is referred to as common sense. I tend to use them interchangeably, but wisdom seems to invoke a profound sense of understanding and awareness. Merriam-Webster's Dictionary distinguished between the two words. It described wisdom as "[implying] sense and judgment far above average."

In contrast, it described common sense as "[suggesting] an average degree of such ability without sophistication or special knowledge" (Merriam-Webster.com. Merriam-Webster, 2019. Web. 10 June 2019). Based on the two definitions, common sense is deemed common understanding without previous or specialized knowledge. Wisdom is considered as above average judgment. If wisdom alone denotes the possession of above-average decision-making, ponder how much more insight can be gained from godly wisdom.

Wisdom appears to be a small thing. Yet investment in it yields unfathomable returns.

Application: Memorize or keep scriptures handy that speak to situations you are dealing with. Refer to those sources of wisdom to remind yourself how to respond in times of conflict. Adopt a growth mindset. It will set you up for being more open to change in your way of processing and cultivate a teachable spirit willing to accept wisdom even in uncomfortable predicaments.

Prayer: Father, give me divine wisdom and insight to guide my decisions. Prepare my heart and show me what it means to have a teachable spirit. In Jesus' name, amen.

Day Thirteen

Self-Discipline Creates Stability

Scriptures: "A truly wise person uses few words; a person with understanding is even-tempered" (Proverbs 17:27, NLT).

"Sensible people control their temper; they earn respect by overlooking wrongs" (Proverbs 19:11, NLT).

Observation: I rarely see people who exhibit the trait of self-discipline suffer from drama and chaos. Or rather they don't frequently suffer from drama and chaos that is self-inflicted.

Living a sensible life may seem underrated. Yet the amount of peace it yields is invaluable. One of the ways to create a more simplistic lifestyle is to demonstrate self-discipline. For instance, eating, spending, and working habits are examples of areas people struggle to operate in self-discipline. But I get it. I live in Louisiana, and the food is good; therefore, as I've gotten older, I've had to rein in my appetite. Metabolisms aren't meant to burn off excess calories forever.

I find joy in efficiency, and I'm able to maintain high levels of productivity through self-discipline.

Application: Become more organized and establish routines to maintain your self-discipline. Even reach out to a trusted friend and ask him or her to keep you accountable to your goals. We all need encouragement, and there is power in unity.

Prayer: Father, create in me a desire for self-discipline. Please, bring to my attention habits, thoughts, and even people who are contributing to the chaos and confusion in my life. I need Your strength to move forward and maintain accountability for my actions. Please, give me the wisdom to know who is deserving of my trust and who is not. In Jesus' name, amen.

Day Fourteen

Resisting Temptation

Scriptures: "No temptation has overtaken you except what is common to mankind. And God is faithful; He will not let you be tempted beyond what you can bear. But when you are tempted, He will also provide a way out so that you can endure it" (1 Corinthians 10:13).

"Anyone who meets a testing challenge head-on and manages to stick it out is mighty fortunate. For such persons loyally in love with God, the reward is life and more life. Don't let anyone under pressure to give in to evil say, 'God is trying to trip me up.' God is impervious to evil and puts evil in no one's way" (James 1:12-13, MSG).

"So, let God work His will in you. Yell a loud no to the devil and watch him scamper. Say a quiet yes to God and He'll be there in no time. Quit dabbling in sin. Purify your inner life. Quit playing the field. Hit bottom and cry your eyes out. The fun and games are over. Get serious, really serious. Get down on your knees before the Master; it's the only way you'll get on your feet" (James 4:7-10, MSG).

Observation: I felt self-discipline preceding resisting temptation was appropriate. Self-discipline directly feeds into resisting temptation. It's foolish to believe we can combat the wiles of this world without fortifying ourselves. Besides, self-discipline, guarding ourselves, and avoiding questionable situations are other ways to resist temptation. Cultivating wisdom and discernment will assist you in spotting those pitfalls from a distance. Then, you can adjust yourself accordingly.

Outside of sheer practicality, a person must realize the power available through the Holy Spirit. We're given strength and wisdom by the Holy Spirit to fight against and resist temptation.

Donning the full Armor of God each morning is critical. I shudder to imagine life without the Holy Spirit, guiding my steps and the Armor of God shielding me from forces meant to harm me.

Application: Begin each morning in prayer, specifically covering the day for you and your loved ones. Pray the full Armor of God as you walk throughout your day. Keep scriptures posted to remind you of promises from God to maintain your joy and peace. Speak scriptures to denounce any lies the enemy is telling you to draw you into depression, despair, and temptation.

Prayer: Father, I plead the Blood of Jesus over myself and my loved ones today. Please bring love, joy, and peace to our spirits. Bring back to our remembrance your everlasting promises. I pray my feet will be fitted with the preparation of the Gospel of Peace; my waist girded with the Belt of Truth; my heart guarded by the Breastplate of Righteousness; my mind protected by the Helmet of Salvation; please lift my arms to carry and hold firm the Shield of Faith that extinguishes the fiery darts of the enemy. I cut through lies and deceptions with the Sword of the Spirit, which is the Word of God. Lord, help me to always fervently pray in the Spirit, making all my requests known to You. In Jesus' mighty name, amen!

Day Fifteen

Joy and Faith Create Synergy

Scriptures: "And we know that in all things God works for the good of those who love Him, who have been called according to His purpose" (Romans 8:28, NIV).

"May the God of hope fill you with all joy and peace as you trust in Him, so that you may overflow with hope by the power of the Holy Spirit" (Romans 15:13, NIV).

Observation: It is overwhelming to create joy while wading through the dregs of daily setbacks. Yet our faith jump-starts a small ray of joy, which bubbles outward into an overflow of abundance. By the same token, joy steadily powers our faith; the positive outlook we need to maintain faith in things unseen is often driven by joy.

Joy and faith have a synergy. You will rarely find one without the other. They feed into each other and reap the benefits of a mutualistic relationship.

When in doubt, build your faith. Joy is sure to breakthrough. If you're down and out, speak God's promises of joy, and watch your faith grow. Joy is resilient, and faith is not affected by trivialities or deterred. Together they are a powerful defense.

Application: Call out the things you are grateful for in your life. You may have to do it several times a day. The purpose is to establish a pattern. Patterns create habits; habits are not easily forgotten. By restoring your joy, you will find the strength to have faith for things even when what you see is a blurry representation of what is to come.

Prayer: Father, I declare and decree joy and faith over myself. I refuse to wallow in pity or setbacks. I prefer to focus my sights on the glory that is to come. My spirit will speak joy even in confusion because I have faith in the unseen. I am grateful for my future testimony. In Jesus' name, amen.

Day Sixteen

Fasting

Scriptures: 1 Corinthians 7:5, ESV, Daniel 10:3, NLT, Isaiah 58:3-7, ESV

"'Even now,' declares the Lord, 'return to Me with all your heart, with fasting and weeping and mourning.' Rend your heart and not your garments. Return to the Lord your God, for He is gracious and compassionate, slow to anger and abounding in love, and He relents from sending calamity" (Joel 2:12-13, NIV).

Observation: There are so many negative connotations associated with fasting. I must admit to occasionally cringing when I hear the word.

Fasting frees the spirit, mind, and body. It strips away all distractions and empties us of unnecessary concerns. It cleanses and allows us to be more receptive to God's voice and His holy presence.

Low points are not meant to break you. Allow yourself to take joy in the opportunity for cleansing. Embrace the chance for a 'reset.'

Application: Reflect on how fasting can discipline any unchecked habits or habits detrimental to your growth. Fasting is different for each person. One person's struggle may not be another person's struggle. Do not feel discouraged if you struggle to break free of a harmful habit while your peer has no difficulties walking in freedom. Our walks with the Lord will vary, which includes the bad with the good. Be gentle with yourself.

Prayer: Father, help me to be honest with You and myself about the areas and things I am struggling with. Through fasting and prayer, I believe by faith; You will give me the victory over them. In Jesus' mighty name, amen.

Day Seventeen

Fostering a Clear Conscience and Transparency

Scriptures: "People with integrity walk safely, but those who follow crooked paths will be exposed" (Proverbs 10:9, NLT).

"The godly hate lies; the wicked cause shame and disgrace" (Proverbs 13:5, NLT).

"People may be pure in their own eyes, but the Lord examines their motives" (Proverbs 16:2, NLT).

Observation: Perfectionism often leads to hypercriticism, which is either focused outward towards others or inward towards ourselves. It can create deep-seated guilt and even shame when we do not live up to high expectations.

In those moments of self-deprecation, we may end up creating a mask. We may go so far as to form a veil of sorts to cover what is truly transpiring in our lives.

The goal may be to live outside of judgment from others; the lies and deceptions burden us instead of freeing us. Not only that, but it also puts us at odds with God and His commandment for righteousness.

Walking in the truth of your situation forms a clear, unburdened conscience. Even if it may not live up to rising expectations, you'll sleep easy at night.

Application: Focus on the things you have accomplished, not the work yet to be completed. The glass half full is the best way to consider the tasks you would still like to finish. Speak the truth. Turn from weaving falsehoods. Living in transparency is freeing and unstressed. Maintaining a lie is more trouble than it's worth.

Prayer: Father, give me the boldness to walk in my truth. Reveal to me the power and freedom that comes with living a life of transparency. In Jesus' name, amen.

Day Eighteen

There is Power in Words

Scriptures: "Some people make cutting remarks, but the words of the wise bring healing" (Proverbs 12:18, NLT).

"Careful words make for a careful life; Careless talk may ruin everything" (Proverbs 13:3, MSG).

"A gentle answer deflects anger, but harsh words make tempers flare. The tongue of the wise makes knowledge appealing, but the mouth of a fool belches out foolishness" (Proverbs 15:1-2, NLT).

"The tongue can bring death or life; those who love to talk will reap the consequences" (Proverbs 18:21, NLT).

Observation: God speaking the universe into existence should be evidence enough of the power of words. Whether we are encouraging others or ourselves, words hold weight and cannot be easily amended once released. Wisdom is paramount when conversing with the people around us. Each person is unique and uniquely affected by their environment. Be careful of the added impact of miscommunications or even thoughtless communication. It can have lasting effects.

Romans 4:17 states we should speak things that aren't as though they were. It means what we internally desire must be released through verbal confirmation, solidifying our faith in what we believe is possible. If we want something to occur or want to make something official, speak those words; otherwise, we have not fully consented.

If you want anything to manifest, you must believe it is possible and speak it, repeatedly if necessary, until possibility becomes a reality.

Application: Write down what you are speaking /declaring by faith. Also, keep a list of words of affirmation to speak over yourself to combat any discouragement you may feel as you wait. It takes patience to wait for the things you believe in.

Prayer: Father, give me patience and unshakable faith to believe even when I cannot see. Please help me to be aware of the weight of my words and use wisdom whenever I speak. I do not want to cause anyone else to fall or become discouraged, so please guide my words and actions. In Jesus' name, amen.

Day Nineteen

Your Body is a Temple

Scriptures: "Anyone who loves to quarrel loves sin..." (Proverbs 17:19, NLT)

"Don't copy the behavior and customs of this world, but let God transform you into a new person by changing the way you think. Then you will learn to know God's will for you, which is good and pleasing and perfect" (Romans 12:2, NLT)

"But he was pierced for our rebellion, crushed for our sins. He was beaten so we could be whole. He was whipped so we could be healed" (Isaiah 53:5, NLT).

Observation: Why do we fail to consistently make our wellbeing a priority? We focus so heavily on everyday survival and our nine-to-five to the point we lose sight of what we need to thrive.

Instead, grow in awareness of self. Understand what covertly or overtly is causing damage to your body and your soul. It is easy to identify physical abnormalities. It is more complicated to locate what plagues our spirit.

Commandments are not in place to take away our freedom. In actuality, they enable us to live in fullness. We understand the logic behind traffic laws; therefore, seek to operate in the spiritual and logical principles behind God's commandments.

Application: Redirect your thoughts and efforts into actions yielding productive results. For instance, being mindful of your thought life and separating yourself from hopelessness.

Always remember, what is best for you will not be best for everyone. Use the methods suited to you while you run your race.

Prayer: Father, I know I will never be perfect. With Your strength, I won't have to struggle alone. Please bring restoration and healing to every area of my being. Give me the self-discipline to care for my body and honor it as God's temple. In Jesus' name, amen.

Day Twenty

Memories Can Sustain or Drain Us

Scriptures: "Each heart knows its bitterness, and no one else can fully share its joy" (Proverbs 14:10, NLT).

"A cheerful heart is good medicine, but a broken spirit saps a person's strength" (Proverbs 17:22, NLT).

"No, dear brothers and sisters, I have not achieved it, but I focus on this one thing: Forgetting the past and looking forward to what lies ahead" (Philippians 3:13, NLT).

"Instead, let the Spirit renew your thoughts and attitudes" (Ephesians 4:23, NLT).

Observation: A fond memory can inspire joy. A dreaded memory can create pervasive fear. When I find myself focusing too much on a memory, dissecting, and analyzing it, I struggle to live in the present moment. On the contrary, a cherished memory causes me to feel lighter, unburdened and empowered. The latter memories are the ones capable of sustaining us in seasons of waiting and seasons of hardships.

Don't throw away the harsh memories. They are reminders of that which we dare not repeat. Just don't allow those memories to overcome and drown you in sorrow. Allow the love flowing from your treasured memories to lift you above any and all adversity.

Life is a cacophony of experiences. Do not allow the harshness of life's realities to outshine the radiance of its blessings.

Application: Photo albums may have become a thing of the past, but visually recording memories have not. Whether you keep digital photos saved to a jump drive or upload them to the cloud, retain some form of tangible reminders. Look for opportunities to share your experiences, too. When we encourage others with our testimonies, we simultaneously encourage ourselves.

Prayer: Father, please help me to keep a fresh perspective of the past. The good and the bad are what have shaped me into the person I am. They do not have to define my worth or become reminders of my failures. Please help me to be strengthened by the good and learn from the bad. In Jesus' name, amen.

Day Twenty-One

Tears are for Cleansing

Scriptures: "He gathers up your tears and puts them in a bottle" (Psalm 56:8).

"No matter how much of your anguish goes unnoticed by others, not one moment escapes the attention of the God who neither sleeps nor slumbers" (Psalm 121:4).

"Those who sow with tears will reap with songs of joy. Those who go out weeping, carrying seed to sow, will return with songs of joy, carrying sheaves with them" (Psalm 126:5, NIV).

Observation: Crying as a reaction to a situation, be it good or bad, normally brings discomfort to the onlooker. Awkwardly, the other person tries to placate the one in distress. It's painful to watch. If you're untrained, dealing with another person's grief is anxiety-inducing. It can be doubly overwhelming if you are the person grieving. Yet there is hope. God sees and numbers every one of our tears.

At one point in my life, I experienced an event that left me in a mourning cycle. Every time I thought I had made progress, the cycle would be triggered again by something or someone. After constantly crying for hours on end, I ran out of tears. My puffy, bloodshot eyes could produce no more tears. I had no choice but to enter the healing process. That is when God met me where I was. I was not rushed to feel whole. I was not made to feel guilty for not moving past my anguished thoughts as quickly as the people around me thought I should have. God kept me and comforted me. I was given a loving and supportive space to embrace what had happened to me and release it at a pace best suited for me.

Things will not pan out perfectly. We have to adapt and overcome. The beauty in the imperfections of life experiences is that none of it is in vain or unseen. Remember, your tears are never wasted. "[What you] sow in tears, [you will reap in] joy" (Psalm 126:5).

Application: Make an intentional effort to allow yourself to feel emotions deeply and imperfectly. Do not be afraid to shed tears. They are not a sign of weakness. They are a sign your heart beats and feels. They are a sign you can begin to heal. Whether you seek relief from prayer or through professional counseling, do not feel burdened to react the way others say you should. It is your life and your experiences.

Prayer: Father, please continue to lift me and carry me as I grieve. Lord, please help me to heal on my timetable and accept what I cannot change. May each tear bring freedom and release from what is binding me. In Jesus' name, amen.

Thanks

God has given me a persistent, sometimes unbearable, unction to write. It is one of the things I know He has commanded me to do. It has led to helping others and myself. I've honestly benefited more from it than my readers. It is a ministry that seeks to encourage others, yet I walk away from it even more encouraged than the people I've ministered to. Our gifts will make room for us. In turn, they will also grant us healing if we are faithful with what He has entrusted to us. So, thank you, God, for trusting me with such a powerful weapon. Words have power!

I would be remiss if I did not thank my mother for her constant promptings to write. Along with my grandmother and maternal aunt, who have been two of my strongest supporters (I will eternally owe them a high debt), my mother has nurtured me in a way only an artist can nurture another artist. She has the clearest understanding of parenthood I've ever seen. I was strong-willed as a child. She knew to appeal to my logic. I was introverted, but people mislabeled me shy. She knew I wasn't shy and wouldn't allow me to feel stigmatized by the label. She supported me in sharing my talents with the world. She knew to bend my will. She didn't want to break it and, in turn, kill my spirit. She was intentional with preserving who I was. Thank you, Momzy, for being patient, even during those times when I spun my wheels haphazardly, desperately trying to find traction.

Oh, and thank you, my itty-bitty sister, Danielle. Since you were able to reach a stove, you've cooked me innumerable delicacies. I know your meals are expressions of your love. We've grown to trust and depend on each other as sisters should.

Special thanks and gratitude to Bianca Chandler and Jillian Dunne for assisting me with the finished product. You ladies are awesome. May God bless your giving hearts.

About the Author

Cassidy is an educator, librarian, freelancer, but most importantly a worker in the kingdom of God. She is a bookworm who loves to travel, dance, create, is a voice actor, gamer, and enjoys spending time with her family and friends.

Developing a fondness for teaching while serving her community through diverse volunteer programs, Cassidy has worked in the field of education in various capacities for 14 years. Previously, she has served on leadership teams and overseen school-wide writing and literacy programs on multiple occasions at several schools' sites for over five years. Cassidy serves youth and children's ministry by teaching a class of 2nd graders and leading a small group/Bible study for young ladies. She was also a part of East Baton Rouge Parish School System's first cohort of technology integration learning leaders and served as the director of a specialty resource library for educators for two years.

Her educational background includes: A Master of Science in Library and Information Studies from Florida State University and a Bachelor of Arts degree in English Liberal Arts from Southern University and A&M College. She holds certifications in 6th-12th grade English, language arts, and reading as well as library media. Currently, she is a doctoral student studying curriculum and instruction through the University of South Carolina's distance education program.

She hopes her dedication will continue to meet the growing needs of educators and students.

Please follow her social media accounts and website for updates here:
https://linktr.ee/cassidyalee

COMING SOON

DREAMSPACE: A COLLECTION OF CREATIVE WORKS

December 2020

CROSS VIEW

December 2021

40-DAY DEVOTIONAL: ABSTAINING AND EMPATHY

June 2022

FLAMES OF ENDURANCE

December 2022

Follow my social media accounts and website for updates here:
https://linktr.ee/cassidyalee

www.ingramcontent.com/pod-product-compliance
Lightning Source LLC
Chambersburg PA
CBHW051412290426
44108CB00015B/2263